Original title:
A Garden Indoors

Copyright © 2025 Creative Arts Management OÜ
All rights reserved.

Author: Colin Leclair
ISBN HARDBACK: 978-1-80581-890-8
ISBN PAPERBACK: 978-1-80581-417-7
ISBN EBOOK: 978-1-80581-890-8

Flourishing Underneath the Eaves

In pots they sit, a wild parade,
The herbs are laughing, they're not afraid.
Tomatoes whisper, 'We love the light!'
While peas insist, 'We're quite the sight!'

The orchids plot while daisies jest,
'Watch out for snails, they're quite the pest!'
With every bloom, they strike a pose,
While cat snoozes, in soft repose.

The Charms Within the Walls

A cactus winks and shares a grin,
While ivy sneaks in from the bin.
Chives communicate by doing a dance,
While ferns giggle at their chance!

The potting soil starts to hum,
As little sprouts give cheeky thumbs.
Bright marigolds trade tales at night,
Claiming they're simply out of sight!

Soft Lullabies of Leaves

A worm provides a nightly show,
While velvet leaves begin to blow.
Moonlight's glow upon their face,
 Singing softly, 'What a place!'

Pots create a cozy nook,
As everybody starts to cook.
The basil tosses leaves with flair,
Declaring, 'Nothing can compare!'

Nurtured by Hands and Dreams

The sun-kissed daisies bask and play,
As potted plants dream the day away.
A watering can sings with pride,
While radishes giggle, 'We're bona fide!'

In this retreat, the colors clash,
A vibrant mess, a quirky splash.
With every touch, they seem to cheer,
'Indoor magic happens here!'

Verdant Views from Window Ledges

Tiny leaves dance in sunlight's glow,
Potted plants strike poses, row by row.
When the cat comes leaping, it's quite a sight,
They pretend to be statues, avoiding the fright.

Dust bunnies dodge as I chase my dreams,
While green friends chuckle in quiet screams.
Whispers of veggies grow wild and free,
They plotted a heist, but forgot the key!

Nature's Embrace in Each Room

My cactus is prickly, but don't take that hard,
It just needs a hug, low-watered and charred.
The ferns hold meetings to strategize plans,
To take over the fridge — those cheeky green fans!

Sunflowers tilt like they're gossiping loud,
While I trip over pots in a plant-parent crowd.
A rogue spider hangs out, great at web games,
We're all one big circus, but no one's to blame!

Roots of Comfort

A rubber plant sprawls, claiming my chair,
Leaves flailing wildly, without a care.
The geraniums giggle, they wear silly hats,
While my bonsai tree looks like a bunch of bats!

I swear the herbs have started a band,
Basil on guitar, while parsley takes stand.
Mint shouts for solo, while rosemary hums,
Who knew my green friends were such little bums?

Tending to Tranquility

In my indoor jungle, I take out the broom,
But the plants just laugh, claiming their room.
'You're the one who watered too much last week!'
They tease with their leaves, such a cheeky sneak.

A wandering spider makes a web of delight,
Caught in my hair, it gives me a fright.
"Should we charge for tours?" thundered the vine,
As I sip my tea, feeling simply divine!

The Sanctuary of Green Within

Chasing dust bunnies, I find some thyme,
A rogue basil, thriving, plotting its crime.
My cat takes a leap, lands right in the pot,
Now I'm pruning parsley, at least that's my thought.

The lavender whispers, 'Please water me next,'
While the cactus just quips, 'I'm feeling perplexed.'
The spider plants dance, knitting tales in the air,
And my fern rolls its eyes as if it doesn't care.

Hidden Eden Beneath the Beams

Under the beams, where no sun ever shines,
A jungle of chaos, mixed with some wines.
On Monday, it's lettuce, on Tuesday, it's sage,
By Wednesday, my zucchini is the center stage.

The herb pots have laughter, a merry old band,
While my succulents argue about who's more grand.
The violets are gossiping—oh, such a racket,
While carrots in silence, have all made a packet.

Fragrant Corners and Starlit Nights

In corners, the mint takes a sneaky, sly peek,
While the geraniums gossip, oh the things that they speak.
Are they planning a heist? Well, not on my watch,
Or they're just chatting while I find a new pot.

The night brings a glow, as my plants start to snore,
With dreams of the wild and adventures galore.
Do they plot for a trip outside, under the moon?
Or scheme to revolt, for a larger commune?

The Living Art of Indoor Life

Canvas of colors splashed everywhere,
With paintbrushes swaying in warm, gentle air.
This art exhibit's got soil and some fun,
With pops of bright petals, oh look, here comes sun!

The daisies critique the way sunflowers smile,
While orchids just scoff and flash their green style.
Each leaf is a canvas, each root tells a tale,
In this vibrant display, we all seem to sail.

A Symphony of Soil and Light

In a pot so round, my peace plants sigh,
They dance in the breeze as I walk by.
The cacti poke fun with their prickly might,
While ferns giggle softly, basking in light.

A tulip tried singing, but croaked out a tune,
The daffodil blushed, said, "Not in June!"
The basil's in charge of the dinner's delight,
Chopping and stirring until late at night.

Oh, but the weeds, they just won't quit,
They crash every party with glee and wit.
I pull them in jest, but they laugh away,
Sipping on sunlight as they dance and sway.

Flourish and Flour

A mint once claimed it was a chef,
Mixing up magic, oh what a theft!
The thyme just rolled its eyes in disdain,
"You're not cooking, you're just a pain!"

The flour in the kitchen took up a pose,
Puffed out its chest as the oven arose.
"I bake the best bread! Just watch me rise!"
But then it got distracted by flour-dusted pies.

The sugar joined in, spreading sweet cheer,
While spices debated who'd be the seer.
Together they giggled till dawn's early light,
Making pancakes of dreams, such a silly sight!

Tiny Ecosystems at Home

Inside this small pot, a jungle's been born,
With germinating seeds that just can't be sworn.
The spider plants plot, all webbed in delight,
While ladybugs laugh, planning a late-night flight.

The ants held a meeting, all dressed in black,
Declaring each leaf a very strong snack.
They marched in a line, a parade quite absurd,
As I yelled, "Hey! You've got some nerve, little nerds!"

The soil held secrets, deep, dark and sly,
Whispering softly, "Join us and fly!"
But I'll stay down here, with a sip of tea,
While it throws a rave for a family of bees!

Where Nature Meets Shelter

In corners and nooks, there's greenery sprouting,
With vines on the ceiling, they're all quite snouting.
The fern strutted boldly, a true fashion star,
"Look at my fronds, I've come from afar!"

A rubber plant claimed it could wear a cape,
Defending the room as it tried to escape.
The violets chuckled, comparing their hats,
While snails composed songs—all about rats!

The flowerpots giggled over tea and crumpets,
Telling wild tales of their humid mishaps.
Where leaves greet each other with flair and with fun,
This indoor party has only just begun!

Enchanted Nooks

In corners where the cacti dance,
A tiny gnome gives plants a chance.
He whispers jokes to ferns and thyme,
  While ivy vines unwind in rhyme.

The soil sings a silly song,
As pots have parties, all night long.
The daisies wear their crowns with pride,
  While succulents attempt to slide.

A peeking snail, a curious guest,
Thinks broccoli's the very best.
With every sprout, a giggle grows,
In cozy spots where green stuff knows.

Oh, what a sight—let's paint the room!
With laughter spills like fresh bouquet bloom.
In every nook, the fun comes alive,
  Indoor blooms on a whim will thrive.

Botanical Dreams at Dusk

As shadows stretch and night creeps in,
The leafy folks begin to grin.
A basil plant starts shaking lights,
While mint pulls pranks with tiny bites.

The daisies wear their sleepy caps,
Telling tales to snoozing snaps.
A fern-like whisper floats through air,
While aloe gives the sun a glare.

Lisa's laughing—who turned off the sun?
The succulents say, 'Let's have some fun!'
With every sprig, a midnight cheer,
As indoor blooms embrace the sphere.

The petals sway, the snickers blend,
In floral realms where joy transcends.
So close your eyes and feel the tune,
With leafy laughter beneath the moon.

The Silence of Potted Peace

In pots where peace and plants entwine,
A cactus whispers, 'Just sip some wine.'
While orchids yawn and start to tease,
   'We grow best in humorous breeze.'

The rubber plant is quite the sage,
With wisdom wrapped in leafy age.
And when it rains, the herbs all dance,
   Creating a botanical romance.

'Why do peppers never play?
Because they can't too hotly sway!'
The flowers chuckle, a giggly crew,
In tranquil depths, life blooms anew.

Yet in the stillness, laughter looms,
As potted friends share funny blooms.
A riot wrapped in plant decor,
   In silent joy forevermore.

Leaves that Listen

In leafy nooks where secrets hide,
The orchids plot with minimal pride.
With gentle sways, they start to laugh,
As every stem becomes a staff.

'What did the fern say to the tree?
Let's branch out—just you and me!'
A giggle echoes through the room,
As potted pals begin to bloom.

Herbs band together, oh what a scene,
'Kale doesn't want to be green, you mean?'
They chuckle softly, slip into cheer,
A flourishing squad, year after year.

So gather 'round and join the show,
For leaves that listen always know.
In their world of fun and verdant play,
Indoor joy finds its leafy way.

Pebbles and Petals

Tiny stones in pots, oh what a sight,
They giggle at flowers, making the night bright.
Each petal's a dancer twirling with glee,
Insisting they shine like stars on the sea.

Cacti in corners, trying to blend,
With cheeky little daisies that twist and bend.
A little worm wiggles to join the parade,
In this humorous chaos, a masterpiece made.

A Tapestry of Growth

In the corner, a fern with a not-so-fresh 'do,
Complains to a succulent that it needs more glue.
The vines tell old tales of stretching too far,
While the herbs snicker, they'd rather be a star.

With petals all gossiping over a cup,
Marigolds laugh till the lights go up.
This wacky ensemble in pots piled high,
Resources are waning, but spirits can't die.

Awakening Green

A sleepy friend sprouts with a yawn and a stretch,
While tulips make bets on the colors they fetch.
A sloppy old watering can joins in the fun,
Spraying the cat who just wanted sun.

A gang of green peas start sharing their dreams,
Of hopping to gardens and sunlit beams.
With shrieks of delight, they wiggle in glee,
Planning their escape – oh, vegetable spree!

Rooted Reflections

Reflecting in puddles, a leafy brigade,
Chortling and chuckling, their worries displayed.
A carrot in denial claims it's a stick,
While blossoms conspire with each little trick.

Basil's got jokes, but it can't quite take root,
While mint rolls its eyes and kicks off its boot.
In this playful refuge, laughter can bloom,
Creating a world where oddities loom.

Cradled in Clay

In pots with dirt, we plant our dreams,
Little sprouts peek out, or so it seems.
Water drips, and soil flies,
Mice take cover, oh, what a surprise!

Cacti joke on tinier sprigs,
"We're the tough guys!" they dance in digs.
Daffodils wear hats of sun,
Saying, "We party while you run!"

The herbs all gossip with leafy glee,
"Who knew being green could be so free?"
While parsnips plot a spicy scheme,
Cousins in salads, a crunchy dream!

But when the cat comes prancing in,
He swears he won't make us thin.
Yet soil's like confetti everywhere,
Indoor adventures, with fluffy flair!

Nature's Canvas in Closed Spaces

Canvas walls, we paint with greens,
Leaves brush against our cereal scenes.
Sunlight peeks through vinyl blinds,
A masterpiece, of laughing minds.

Potatoes giggle under their masks,
Saying, "Who knew we'd make gourmet tasks?"
Spinach winks in the corner's light,
"Eat us raw, we dare you, take a bite!"

Pansies plotting in bright array,
"Who knew dirt could be so cliché?"
The garden gnomes look quite bemused,
In our small realm, they feel so used.

But as the evening rounds its end,
Nature's whispers are the best blends.
With laughter sprouting in every crevice,
Who knew indoor greens could feel so reckless?

A Ray of Green Light

In window nooks where shadows play,
Tiny leaves dance and sway,
Reaching for the sun above,
Saying, "We're deserving of love!"

The fern laughs, tickling our toes,
While Ivy drapes like a boss of prose.
Sycamores in vases blink,
"Is this a jungle, or just a sink?"

Succulents cracking up in rows,
"Too tough for you? Look how it grows!"
Ficus trees wear beards of dust,
Hoping they survive this indoor bust.

But when the vacuum starts to hum,
The plants all tremble, making a thrum.
Yet in this chaos, blooms ignite,
A ray of joy, oh what a sight!

Sanctuary of Silhouettes

In the evening light, we gather here,
Plants disguise like spies, oh dear!
Shadows stretching on the wall,
"Who's the tallest?" they all call.

A prickly pear gives a cheeky grin,
"Go on, blush—it's my favorite sin!"
While snake plants plot in steady rows,
"Let's cozy up when chaos grows!"

The soil whispers, "Keep it down,"
As herbs exchange their royal crown.
Green mischief lurks in every pot,
Who knew life could be so hot?

But as we sip our lemon tea,
These shades of green are wild and free.
In this indoor realm of fun and jest,
We've found a place that feels so blessed!

Echoes of the Forest Inside

In the corner, a fern looks sly,
Telling secrets with a little lie.
"Water me not, or I will pout!"
It's really just looking for a sprout.

A cactus beams, brags every day,
"I've got the spikes; they keep foes away!"
But when a fly dares to buzz too close,
It's really quite afraid, like a timid ghost.

The pot with herbs has a party vibe,
Sage and thyme, they're on a jive!
"Let's cook together, it's a total blast,"
Says the basil, while hoping it won't be the last.

A pebble path winds through this scene,
Where vegetables dance, oh so keen!
It's a riot of flavors, a silly spree,
Where the greens do the tango and the peas are free!

Nurtured Wilderness within Our Walls

In the living room, a narrow tree,
Does its best to reach for me.
"Hey! I'm the tallest here, can't you see?"
While I just chuckle, sipping my tea.

A cheeky spider spins a web,
Learning to dance, now that's its celeb!
It shakes with pride on its little perch,
While I pretend to switch my search.

The succulents strut, oh so bold,
But in a drought, their charm's grown cold.
"Just give us light, and not too much cheer!"
As they bicker for sun like kids at school here.

In each nook, there's a quirky crew,
With a talking soil that dreams of dew.
They laugh at the dust while plotting their schemes,
Turning this home into whimsical dreams!

Planted Joy in the Heart of Dwellings

Potting soil had quite the chat,
With a rogue worm who wore a hat.
"Let's dig together and make a mess!"
And turned the carpet into a dress!

The lavender whispers, "I smell so fine!"
While the mint adds, "Better pour some wine!"
But the rosemary shushes, "It's time for tea!"
And they all giggle, feeling so free.

A daisy in the window goes punk,
With petals askew, it strikes a funk!
"Style is key, don't you agree?"
While the Snapdragon bubbles with glee.

Together they plot a floral parade,
With pots preparing for the big charade.
In this festive realm, joy's always planted,
And the house sings tunes quite enchanted!

Whispers of the Houseplant

In the shadows, a philodendron sighs,
"Why is my friend the cactus so high?"
While the aloe grins with gooey pride,
"I'm the one that they can't deny!"

The pothos stretches, a lazy sort,
Clinging to walls for the fun of sport.
"Watch me swing and sway today,"
As it pulls off stunts in a bright display.

The jade plant tells tales of wealth,
"Just water me gently, I'll find good health!"
But the eager spider plant just rolls,
"I'm the one that's filling all the holes!"

So here they chatter, as day turns to night,
With leaves that flutter and feelings light.
In this haven, the banter's on cue,
Where every plant shares a laugh or two!

Sanctuary of Green

In a pot sits a tiny sprout,
Whispers secrets, never shouts.
A cactus wearing a party hat,
It thinks it's quite the acrobatic cat.

Ferns hold hands in a leafy dance,
While succulents lounge in a sunlit trance.
Pothos vines swing like they're on a spree,
Who knew plants loved a good cup of tea?

Lush Oasis in Living Rooms

A rubber plant plays peek-a-boo,
While a leafy friend says, "Who are you?"
Spiders spin webs of a playful tale,
As the rubber ducky joins the scale.

Dancing shadows bounce on the wall,
When the sun rises, they have a ball.
The wandering jew just can't stay still,
An indoor rave is brewing—what a thrill!

Shadows of Indoor Blooms

Petunias giggle in shades of pink,
Sunflowers wink, giving us a blink.
A geranium sighs with a heavy heart,
Because the pruner's coming—oh, what a start!

Hiding gnomes throw a secret soiree,
With daisies gossiping, 'What did they say?'
The shadows swirl, teasing the light,
As plants plot to conquer the night!

The Dance of Foliage

Lettuce twirls in a neon pot,
While thyme tries breakdancing, but's just not hot.
Basil shimmies in a fragrant breeze,
In this leafy party, there's no one to tease.

A fiddle leaf fig tries a twist,
But promptly falls—what a funny twist!
The indoor blooms laugh, full of glee,
For in this space, all are carefree!

Vibrant Hues Against Urban Grays

Potted plants dance on windowsills,
Where city sounds don't pay the bills.
Cacti wearing tiny hats and shades,
Plant parties with shimmery parades.

Fern fronds wave as if to say,
"Join us for a leafy holiday!"
Succulents gossip about the sun,
In this concrete jungle, we have fun!

Chlorophyll dreams in late-night chats,
Wondering if they could be cool cats.
Growing tall while we watch in awe,
Who knew plants could break the law?

A tulip's wink, a daisy's grin,
No one's uptight, we're in the spin.
Urban life, you're always a bore,
But in this dappled light, we soar!

Tranquil Moments in Leafy Retreats

In the corner, a spider plant calls,
Throwing shade on those friendship falls.
When life gets loud and thoughts run wild,
A peace lily smiles, ever so mild.

Mossy rocks tell tales of missed trips,
While petunias gossip in their soft grips.
"Let's chill today, ditch the big crowd!"
Sunshine rays burst, fluffy and proud.

Pining for calm in green company,
With herbal tea, it's a remedy.
Laughter spills like water, sweet and light,
In our plush retreat, all feels right.

We share secrets in leaf-laden oaths,
In pots that cradle the best of growths.
Who knew joy blooms in such cozy nooks?
These leafy friends write my favorite books!

Secrets Sown in Indoor Soils

Plant pots whisper secrets at night,
While I sip tea and ponder delight.
Napping ferns peek from their green walks,
Intriguing tales of their root-bound talks.

Basil dreams of Italian nights,
While sage rolls eyes and takes delights.
They plot world fame from kitchen shelves,
Who knew they'd think they were such elves?

Every sprout and bloom has a plan,
To escape their pots, and be a fan.
"Just one stretch, maybe a leap,
From windowsill, we'll have a sweep!"

As they plot, I prune and laugh,
Dancing roots, it's quite the craft.
In this soil, secrets are gold,
Come join the fun, let the tales unfold!

Botanical Dreams from the Comfort Zone

Cactus dreams of sandy beaches,
While lavender instructs how to teach us.
"Let's put the fun in fungus tonight,
And dance with the air plants, all alight!"

An herbivore staggers, lost in thought,
Peeking at mint while seeking what's sought.
Rooftop romances among the leaves,
Zucchini plans stories, and it believes.

In the hum of lights, we'll create a show,
A leafy circus, oh don't be slow!
In this indoors kingdom where we grow,
The chatter is high, and the spirits flow!

Dreams of wild jungles fill the air,
Tropicals whisper, "Life's never bare!"
So gather 'round, let's have some cheer,
In our green nook, there's nothing to fear!

Harvesting Tranquility in a Tiny Space

In pots they grow, like little spies,
Peeking at me with leafy eyes.
I water them, they nod and sway,
Don't ask me why—they just display.

I've lost a plant, it's quite the scene,
Now it's a ghost, but still it's green.
I talk to them, they take their cue,
It's a one-sided chat—what can they do?

I swear the herbs plot on the shelf,
Like they're conspiring to save themselves.
Their whispers mix with my kitchen air,
Every dish a chance to show they care.

So if you find my plants take flight,
Don't fret, they're just seeking sunlight.
In laughter's bloom, we share the space,
My leafy pals—have quite the grace.

Basking in the Glow of Indoor Flora

Sunlight hits them, they look so proud,
Each leaf's a dancer, standing loud.
I catch them smiling, what a sight,
I swear they giggle; it feels so right.

A cactus tries to make a joke,
But with those spines, it's just a poke.
I roll my eyes; they poke back, too,
Indoor wit, who knew it grew?

The ferns are flocking for a rave,
They love the tunes, quite the rave.
Like tiny furs with rhythm beats,
Plant party time, oh what a feast!

And when the dusk arrives to play,
They dream of roots by light of day.
While I sip tea and laugh a bit,
My flora friends are so legit.

Serenity Grown in Planters' Embrace

In cozy corners, pots align,
Chasing the chill with roots divine.
They hum a tune, a calming breeze,
Telling tales of sunny trees.

A fern has taken up the lead,
Directing greens like a plant-based creed.
I wave it off, can't take the helm,
Though it secretly runs this realm!

The peppers joke, 'Let's spice this life!'
While lavender lounges, void of strife.
I swear they giggle—who knew they'd cheer?
A botanical sitcom, right here!

I toss the soil, a muddy dance,
These greens seem to know—a fun romance.
In pots we laugh and grow and play,
Serenity blooms in our array.

The Colorful Pulse of Homegrown Nature

Petunias wink in shades so bright,
Watching me stumble—what a sight!
I tripped on thyme, oh what a blunder,
My indoor maze—more like a wonder!

The tomatoes tell me, 'You wear that green!'
But it's just my shirt, if you know what I mean.
With giggles rustling through the air,
Their jokes are fresh, beyond compare!

The daisies dance like they own the room,
Spreading cheer, they chase the gloom.
In pots they pulse with vibrant glee,
An indoor wildness, just wait and see!

And when the evening starts to call,
They whisper tales, one and all.
Together we laugh, sing, and grow,
In this colorful space, our joy will flow.

Echoes of Garden Aromas

In pots of clay, my herbs do sway,
They dance in sun, though slightly gray.
A basil leaf, it gave a cheer,
"You chop me up? That's rather queer!"

Next door, a cactus tries to smile,
But prickly hugs can be a trial.
I told a fern about my dreams,
It whispered back, "Just work with beams!"

The tomatoes plot up in their beds,
"Let's grow big!" they squabble and spread.
A radish grumbled, "I'm so small!"
"At least you're not a bouncy ball!"

In this indoor space, things may get wild,
With a spider plant who acts like a child.
Each sprout has jokes that never fail,
In this green room, we laugh and sail!

Verdant Heartbeats

A leafy friend named Phil the Thrill,
Keeps growing tall, it's quite a skill.
"I'm on a diet!" said my lace,
"Less sun for me, more thyme in place!"

The sunflower seeks a lofty goal,
To be the tallest—oh, what a troll!
"Watch me reach!" it shouted loud,
But bumped its head, so no high crowd.

The ferns just giggle, oh what fun,
While sneezing mint is on the run.
In this green crew, chaos reigns,
With jokes as wild as happy trains!

Forget the rules, let's have a blast,
These quirky greens, they'll grow so fast!
Each pot a character with a voice,
In our indoor life, we all rejoice!

Indoor Sprouts and Soul

With sprouting beans, my hopes take flight,
They wave their leaves; oh, what a sight!
"I'm growing strong!" the peas declare,
While quietly plotting to take the fair.

An artichoke in splendid green,
Laments it's always stuck unseen.
"Where are my fans?" it sighs and moans,
"Is this the place for leafy drones?"

Chives are laughing, tickling air,
"Our jokes are fresh—come take a share!"
While tomatoes squeeze in a tight race,
"Try ketchup; we're about to chase!"

Together we bloom with silly glee,
In our little corner, wild and free.
Every pot has dreams, it's true,
Our indoor metas bloom anew!

Embracing Nature's Palette

In pots adorned with colors bright,
The orchids laugh and twirl with light.
"We're fancy flowers, can't you see?"
While marigolds just hum with glee.

"I'm a climber!" screams the vine with pride,
But trips on leaves—it can't decide!
A pepper plant teases with a wink,
"My hotness burns, but I can think!"

A cheerful Thai basil sings a tune,
Service without having to moon.
The rosemary rolls in playful cheer,
"Smell my essence, I'm always near!"

With each new sprout, we fill the air,
In this indoor jungle, none compare.
We paint a scene of laughter bold,
A quirky mix of green and gold!

Petals and Shadows: A Room Transformed

In the corner, a cactus dances,
Wobbling slightly with its prickly pants.
A pot of basil sings to the sun,
While a rogue fern plots how to run.

A vase of daisies mocks the cat,
Who thinks she's stealthy, oh, how she's fat!
The orchids giggle, swaying about,
In this room, we've mastered the indoor sprout.

Something's blooming on the kitchen shelf,
But who's to say it's not just myself?
With every splash of vibrant hue,
I laugh, my room's become a zoo.

As shadows dance from the growing light,
I sip my tea, what a silly sight!
Petals whisper secrets of glee,
In my whimsical plant jubilee.

Ferns and Flowers: An Indoor Serenade

Ferns wave their fronds like they're in a band,
While daisies tune up, take a firm stand.
A spider plant plays it cool and sly,
And I wonder who's the lead, oh my!

The violets gossip, oh my, look at him!
That poor little succulent, so pale and dim!
With a little water and some sun's caress,
He'll be dancing soon, no need to guess.

Tulips put on quite the show tonight,
In this lit-up room, everything feels right.
With laughter and petals floating around,
Nature sends its cheer, all glory abounds.

My heart sings thanks for this funky place,
Where every leaf wears a goofy face.
Ferns and flowers, well, what a charade!
This indoor serenade will never fade.

Roots of Serenity in a Concrete Jungle

In a jungle wrought of steel and stone,
A peace lily reigns, proudly sown.
With blossoms bright, it shouts, "Hello!"
While the potted mint gives a cheeky show.

On the windowsill, the thyme chimes in,
"I'm just here for the fun, not to win!"
But down below, those tubers plot,
Spreading their roots in a well-configured spot.

Comical chaos in this oddity,
Whenever guests come, oh, such hilarity!
"Is that a plant or where did you stash
Your crazy aunt's old mustache?"

Amidst the concrete, joy can bloom,
With every quirky plant in this room.
Roots spreading wide in weird ways,
Who knew this life could be such a phrase?

Interior Blooms: Nature's Gentle Touch

In the heart of my home, a bloom takes stage,
With petals like laughter spilling from a page.
A rubber plant squawks, out of its pot,
Claiming it's royalty, silly but hot!

The pothos vine stretches, reaching too far,
Draping over the lamp, looking like a star.
While peace lilies chuckle, staying all neat,
Poking fun at their friends, oh, what a treat!

With each little leaf, there's a story to weave,
Of how they all thrive, and together believe.
Glass jars filled with dirt, oh, the mess is divine,
Laughter erupts—"Here's a rock, it's mine!"

So whisper sweet nothings to petals so bright,
In this colorful chaos, I find pure delight.
With nature's touch, my heart skips a beat,
In this quirky world, life is truly sweet.

Whispers of Leafy Dreams

In a pot sat a fern so proud,
Complaining if it didn't get loud.
"I need more sun, oh can't you see?"
As if it could sip more light for free.

The cactus laughed, with spines so sharp,
"Calm down, pal, it's quite the lark!"
"We're all just here to take up space,"
The orchid winked with bloomy grace.

A rogue basil grew under the sink,
Sassed at the thyme, said, "What do you think?"
"I'm the king in this earthy stew,"
While the mint plotted a hue of blue.

And as I watered with a big, wide grin,
They gossiped about my singing sin.
"Here comes the human with the can!"
Little did they know I had a plan!

The Secret Oasis Beneath the Roof

A lonely palm swayed in delight,
Said, "This kitchen's my nature's sight!"
While a spider plant danced in glee,
"I'm blooming fabulous, just wait and see!"

The dracaena smirked from its nook,
"Fancy being part of a cookbook?"
"Chill out, dude! You're safe from the stew,"
Shrugged the spider plant, "What else is new?"

A fern's whisper snuck through the air,
"Can you keep secrets? I've one to share!"
"I hear the human talks to us all,"
"Yeah, and you once even tried to call!"

They plotted a coup for the light, oh joy,
"I'm definitely the sunniest toy!"
When the room was snug and without a doubt,
Every plant laughed as I walked about.

Sunlight's Embrace in a Room of Verdure

Sunbeams peek through the window's space,
Where every stem dreams of a race.
"I'll catch the light first!" said the chive,
While the lavender whispered, "I'll thrive!"

The jade plant plotted in silence,
"Sunbathing is an art of pure defiance!"
But all the blooms gave a knowing grin,
"Bet you'll wilt if the sun comes in!"

A wanderer tossed a tiny seed,
"No one invited me, indeed!"
"You'll just be another leafy face,"
Said the rosemary with casual grace.

With laughter shared from leaf to leaf,
Inside this jungle, there's no grief.
They chatter on about the day,
While I pay heed to their sassy play.

Sylvan Symphony behind Closed Doors

The fiddle leaf fig had a flair for jazz,
While the pothos vibed with its pizzazz.
"Let's start a band, we're stars tonight!"
As they swayed beneath the bulb's warm light.

Succulents chimed in with a beat,
"We're cooler than the old, dusty fleet!"
"Yeah, but do you know how to groove?"
Each echoed leaf had something to prove.

The peace lily sang a sweet refrain,
"Water me well or I'll go insane!"
While the heartleaf philodendron sneered,
"Lucky for you, my watering's cheered!"

In this vibrant patch, full of flair,
Who needs the outdoors when fun's in the air?
So here we are, each green delight,
Making music in the soft moonlight.

A Home for Tender Roses

In pots they dream of sunny days,
With bright pink blooms in funny ways.
They shake their heads when waters pour,
"We're not fish! Just open the door!"

Each leaf has stories, wild and grand,
Of mud pies made by little hands.
They giggle softly, roots entwined,
A secret club, humor defined.

With sunlight streaming through the glass,
They hold their meetings, none let it pass.
A cactus claims he loves the joke,
"I'm sharp and witty! Just look, I poke!"

When shadows dance, they twirl with glee,
A fern flirts with the bonsai tree.
In this pot party, no one's aloof,
They all get along, proof of their proof.

Sowing Tranquility

Planting seeds in silly rows,
Twitching leaves, a giggling prose.
The daisies snicker, saying, "Hey!"
"We're not flowers, we're here to play!"

The watering can dances too,
With splashes that feel like a debut.
"Splash my roots, I'm ready now!"
Yelled the tulip, wearing a cow.

Growing tall with grand displays,
Laughing in the sun's warm rays.
A broccoli winks, an herb sends cheer,
"All of you, come join here, my dear!"

With the sun setting, they giggle so,
"Tomorrow more seeds, yes, let's grow!"
They close their eyes, a sleepy troop,
In this playful plot, they form a loop.

Urban Flora and Fauna

In concrete jungles, plants break free,
Making mischief, wild as can be!
A leafy monkey hangs upside down,
Swinging over the soft, green crown.

The city lights shine bright at night,
While succulents laugh at their own height.
Drippy ferns play peekaboo,
"Let's make this urban life our zoo!"

A lily pads her way to fame,
Said, "When rain comes, I'll stake my claim!"
Her pet goldfish gives a little swirl,
"Together we'll make this city twirl!"

As pigeons strut, and traffic hums,
The plants join in, their laughter drums.
In pots and smiles, they find their way,
Urban flora, brightening the gray.

Within These Quiet Halls

Within these walls, the leaves converse,
With puns that surely could disperse.
A peace lily hums a comical song,
In tones that make the shadows strong.

The spider plant swings, almost like a dance,
While succulents tease, given the chance.
"We're in the house, let's start a show!"
Yelled the sleepy thyme, "Oh, let's go!"

The light from above makes shadows play,
As laughter spills in a bright ballet.
"Who needs a stage? We have this pot!"
Cried a seedling friend, "We're all that!"

In corners, whispers of fun abound,
Plants tell tales with roots that are sound.
And thus in silence, such chaos grows,
With every petal, the humor flows.

A Symphony of Soil and Sunshine

In pots of clay, a battle rages,
Tiny sprouts in funny stages,
With droopy leaves and dreams of high,
Each one is aiming for the sky.

A watering can, a clumsy dance,
Plants giggle at their second chance,
Sun on the sill, they stretch and yawn,
Whispers of spinach greet the dawn.

Fungus and dirt play hide and seek,
Each little weed, a cheeky freak,
A cactus grins, oh what a tease,
While herbs erupt in fits of sneeze.

So join the fun, let laughter bloom,
In every room, there's nature's loom,
With green confetti 'round the house,
Wait for the day a plant can grouse!

Green Horizons in a Caged Space

In window frames, a jungle grows,
With pots that dance and flowers that pose,
A fern in a hat, is that a joke?
And peppers giggle at the smoke.

A spindly vine has dreams so grand,
Plans to climb and take the land,
Yet knocks a lamp down in the fray,
Who knew it could be such a play?

A rubber plant dons sunglasses bright,
As if it's planning a wild night,
While daisies gossip, quite absurd,
About the secrets plants have heard.

In this small room, the chaos reigns,
Each little leaf, with joy it gains,
So dust off that green thumb, my friend,
Let the indoor silliness never end!

Nature's Refuge Behind our Walls

Behind these walls, green life unfolds,
With stories of sunshine brightly told,
A succulent's smirk, can you believe?
It jokes about the dust it weaves.

A basil bush, with chef's delight,
Whispers recipes late at night,
While ferns do yoga, bending low,
Under the light's soft, glowing show.

A tiny spider plants a scene,
It's caught a fly— oh what a dream!
The beads of moisture dance with glee,
As if they're having a tea party.

With pots as guests and soil as stage,
Each leafy friend, a different age,
We laugh together, what a ball,
In this wild space, we're friends with all!

Botanical Whispers in Cozy Nooks

In corners snug, the greens convene,
In whispered tones, they plot unseen,
A lavender sprig fears the spice,
Too much cinnamon— oh, that's not nice!

The shadows flicker, a herbaceous chat,
As thyme complains, and rosemaries spat,
"Why do we live in this cramped estate?"
"Stop moaning, mate! Let's celebrate!"

Marigold winks at the growing host,
"I'll be the star at tonight's roast!"
The aloe vera, wise and bold,
Says, "Keep it cool, let the stories unfold."

Such life we share, with giggles and grunts,
With soil-stained fingers, we do the hunts,
In each little nook, there's joy and cheer,
Join the plant party, let's raise a beer!

Cultivating Joy in Petal-Laden Rooms

In pots and vases, sprouts do cheer,
A dance of leaves, oh how they leer!
They stretch for light, all green and spry,
While sunbeams giggle from on high.

The herbs conspire in fragrant plots,
Basil whispers, 'I draw the smocks!'
Thyme chuckles soft, 'I'm quite the catch!'
While mint insists, 'I'm here to snatch!'

With little care, the blooms will thrive,
As laughter fills this leafy hive.
Each day's a joke, each petal bright,
While watering can's a laughing sight!

Let's plant some smiles, let's sow the fun,
With every sprout, a little pun.
In every corner, magic's brewed,
In our home oasis, joy is stewed.

Balance of Nature in Enclosed Spaces

In corners, sprouts begin to chat,
'Did you hear? The cat might nap!'
A spider plant swings like a pro,
While peace lilies put on a show.

Cacti quip, 'I'm prickly but neat!'
Ferns flirt around with luscious heat.
Petunias blush in vibrant hues,
While all the fakes sip morning brews.

The air is sweet, a fragrant spree,
As pollen plays hide and seek with glee.
Boxes and pots, a contest for space,
Each leaf a laugh, a leaf a grace.

Nature's trick with a hint of cheer,
In every nook, we spread our cheer.
Tables and shelves, a leafy race,
Foliage giggles in this warm place.

The Color and Calm of Indoor Life

With colors bright, they sing their song,
In playful hues, they all belong.
The orchids wink, the daisies smile,
While ferns sway softly for a while.

Tulips tease with their gentle flair,
Potatoes hide beneath the chair!
A sprinkle here, a sprinkle there,
Our patch of green makes hearts declare.

Spider plants made beds of silk,
Sipping sunlight like warm milk.
Each leaf a tale, each petal a prank,
In indoor life, we find our rank.

As shadows stretch and sunlight bends,
With laughter, nature always blends.
In every crack, and every nook,
A joyful page in our green book.

Stillness Wrapped in Flora and Foliage

In stillness reigns a leafy domain,
Where violets dream and roses feign.
In quiet corners, whispers play,
As hanging plants swing and sway.

Peeking shyly around the bend,
The succulents giggle, they pretend!
'Fiddle leaf, you're getting tall!'
'But I'm the star—await your fall!'

Aroma drifts, a aromatic spree,
While lavender laughs at all, you see.
Wrapped in green, we find our breath,
In every leaf, a little jest.

So here's to flora, full of cheer,
In this snug nook, they hold us dear.
With each green sprout, a tale unfolds,
In stillness, laughter finds its molds.

Blooming Amidst the Walls

In pots they sit, in happy rows,
Each plant a tale that nobody knows.
The cactus teases, 'I never cry,'
While daisies giggle, 'Oh me, oh my!'

The sun peeks in, like a nosy friend,
Watering cans become the weekend trend.
Fern fronds dance like they're in a show,
As ivy whispers, 'Let's put on a glow!'

A spider plant takes a leafy leap,
While rubber trees silently keep.
Basil smells like a pizza party,
Chives strut, thinking they're quite hearty!

Who needs a yard when you've got this spree?
Green companions make the day so free.
With every sprout, my giggles grow,
In this indoor wild, the fun won't slow!

Sanctuary of Leaves

Here in my zone, the greens unite,
They're plotting pranks in the soft moonlight.
A leafy army, all in jest,
A rubber plant thinks it's quite the best!

The herbs conspire for culinary fame,
While orchids flaunt their floral name.
Pothos drapes like it's in a play,
Swaying gently, dancing the day away!

With each new sprout, a giggle grows,
As ferns engage in leafy throes.
The air is thick with mischief galore,
Who knew plants could entertain and more?

In my glass oasis, laughter's delight,
Every leaf joining in the night.
An earthy comedy, ever so close,
In this little space, I'm the happy host!

Homegrown Serenity

I've got thyme on my hands, just you wait,
Mint sips tea, thinks it's quite first-rate.
The basil whispers, 'Let's dance a jig,'
While sage rolls eyes at the humble twig.

Succulents sunbathe, looking quite cool,
While the fern gets tipsy in the pool.
Each sprout giggles at its own height,
Dreaming of growing up overnight!

Chili plants brag about their spice,
While peace lilies play a game so nice.
Pansies prance without any care,
In this indoor space, fun fills the air!

Here in my haven, we all play fair,
Joy blooms softly; it's a leafy affair.
A quirky family of soil and breeze,
Bringing me laughter with effortless ease!

The Language of Ferns

Ferns whisper secrets with every frond,
Telling tales of the backyard beyond.
With leafy giggles, they share their tricks,
While succulents chuckle at gardening flicks.

Bamboo teases, 'I'm tall, what of it?'
While creeping vines hover just a bit.
The soil speaks in a playful tone,
As flowers flirt, feeling quite grown!

Rosemary laughs, 'I'm your savory mate,'
While lavender winks with aromatic fate.
In this pot of antics, the fun runs wild,
Each leaf knows how to be a playful child!

In my plant parade, there's joy to be found,
With each little sprout, hilarity's crowned.
So let them chatter, root, and wend,
In this space of greens, every day transcends!

Traces of Nature's Touch

Little pots stacked high, oh what a sight,
My vines are swinging, causing delight.
The cat's on a mission, climbing the shelves,
Knocking down leaves, is he seeking elves?

With watering can ready, I make my rounds,
Oops! A flood warning, it's raining down sounds.
Splashes and giggles, it's all in the game,
Guess my plants think the bathroom's to blame!

Tiny blooms grumble, 'We want some more sun!'
Pushing their petals, they shout, 'This is fun!'
I swear they've formed a little revolt,
Pouting in soil, it's my hostess fault!

So here we dance in our green little spree,
The plants play along, as wild as can be.
Amidst our laughter, sunlight beams bright,
Indoors, we're cavorting—oh what a sight!

Whispers Among Foliage

In this leafy jungle, secrets abound,
My pothos whispers, 'What's lost can be found.'
The spider plant snickers, it's not hard to see,
They're plotting to cover the TV, oh me!

The succulent winks, 'I hardly need water,'
While ferns raise their fronds, 'We flourish, no slaughter!'

A conversation blooms, it's buzzing with cheer,
While I just stand back, holding snacks near!

Cacti who gossip with arms open wide,
Wonder what plants would think if they tried.
Chasing the sunlight, like kids on the run,
These leafy companions truly know how to have fun!

As I pour more soil, they laugh and conspire,
Giggling in green, their laughter won't tire.
In this midst of chaos, a wild little scene,
Life in a pot, oh, it's weirdly serene!

Earthy Hues and Homey Sights

Colors of green splash painted on walls,
Furrowing brows as the pot finally falls.
The dirt flies high, a miniature spree,
Plants giggling together—just me and my tea!

My basil's a diva, demanding its space,
While thyme's got a crush, oh, what a chase!
Lilies are feuding; it's quite the parade,
Who knew my décor would lead to charades?

I've got a fern trying to reclaim its throne,
While orchids are trading their stories alone.
'This pot is too small,' they whine and they pout,
I'm just the gardener, but feel like a scout!

Yet among all this gossip, there's laughter I hear,
These plants are a riot, my stress disappears.
So I sit in their presence, a witness to glee,
In my colorful home, it's just them and me!

A Touch of Wildness Within

An elephant ear towers, my head in the clouds,
While the jade plant chuckles, all prim and so proud.
Each leaf plays a tune, I swear they can talk,
While I dance with a broom and pretend I can rock!

The rubber tree teases, it's growing so bold,
'Watch out!' it shouts, 'I might make you old!'
I roll my eyes, as they spring back to life,
Amidst all their antics, there's not much strife.

A waltz in the sunlight, the vines intertwine,
My laughter erupts, like some vintage wine.
Who knew indoor plants could bring such a cheer?
With dirt on my hands, I hold nature dear.

So here's to the chaos, the joy, and the fun,
In my wildest of hold, I feel so well done.
Each petal, each stem, a reminder, it's true,
The wildness, the laughter, it all starts with you!

Soft Shadows on the Floor

When leaves pretend to dance with glee,
The cat pounces, thinking it's free.
A pot tipped over, soil on my shoe,
Now I'm a gardener—who knew?

The sun peeks in for a friendly gaze,
Plants giggle softly in a green haze.
A spider weaves webs, a master of art,
But can't catch the dust that flies from the heart.

A cactus complained of a sunburned day,
While the fern just sighed, 'I'm feeling so gray.'
The herbs are chatting, gossiping soft,
As I trip on a watering can, my laugh a scoff.

So here we are, a funny revue,
Of leaves and petals, a laugh or two.
In this indoor jungle, chaos does grow,
But hey, what's that smell? Who stepped on a show?

In the Company of Blooms

There's a rose with a temper, it shouts at the sun,
'Come out, you lazy, have some fun!'
A daisy giggles, 'I don't even care,
I just want to be the one with flair!'

The violets whisper, 'Is that a weed?
It's creeping quite close to our colorful creed!'
And then there's thyme, who's quite the wit,
Says, 'Every moment here is a little bit hit.'

"Why are those leaves drooping?" I question with dread,
"Perhaps too much water," the mint said and fled.
The orchids are plotting a tea party soon,
With sugar and sunlight—no need for a moon!

In this mix of blooms, there's laughter and cheer,
Every petal has something to add, so dear.
A party like this, how could it be wrong?
Turns out, life in here is a boisterous song!

The Breath of Indoor Life

The ficus stands proud, with a leaf-flicking spree,
While the pothos trails down, trying to flee.
The incense stick sighs, 'Please don't take too long,'
While dust bunnies drift, quietly strong.

'These poor lightbulbs, they're dimming so fast!'
Whispers the basil, all fragrant and vast.
The lightbulbs just chuckle, they've seen it all,
Under their glow, the plants have a ball.

The aloe quite cheerfully tells a tall tale,
'Of sun-sprinkled summers while I sail!'
But the peace lily frowns, 'That's not like my vibe.
I prefer quiet with a splash of good jive.'

And so we collide in this lively indoor space,
With laughter and foliage, we share our grace.
Every leaf is a story, a punchline or two,
In this quirky cocoon, where hilarity grew.

Gentle Horizons of Flourishing

Sprouts are peeking, faces so bright,
They ask me, 'Is it morning or night?'
The sun's playing tag with the shadows nearby,
While the lilac just giggles, 'Oh, how time flies!'

The window is open, a breeze comes in low,
And the wheatgrass whispers, 'Let's put on a show!'
The indoor league of the funny and spry,
Every petal has secrets—the best kind, oh my!

"Watch out!" cried the chives, as they teeter and spin,
While the jasmine pipes up, 'Shut your herb hole, win!'
The basil just chuckles, 'I'm spice with a twist,
You all bring the laughs, it's hard to resist!'

So here's to the moments of laughter and green,
In this lively nook where we laugh and preen.
With pots full of joy, it's a humorous game,
In this place of delight, we're never the same!

A Lullaby of Green

In pots they sit, quite snug and round,
With leaves like hats, they dance around.
A cactus hums a sleepy tune,
While ferns pretend to swoon by moon.

Tiny sprouts in a coffee cup,
They want to grow, oh, what a sup!
With each sip, they jump and cheer,
"Don't drink us up, we want to steer!"

The herbs all gossip, green and spry,
"When will the carrots learn to fly?"
While mint dreams of a party place,
And basil laughs, says, "What a grace!"

So nestled in this cozy nook,
They'll stretch and wiggle, cheer by hook.
With laughter bright, they'll softly gleam,
A leafy world, a plant-based dream.

Tendrils of Imagination

In every pot, a tale is spun,
A basil knight with his sword of fun.
The thyme's a wizard, tiny and bold,
Casting spells with tales retold!

Peeking out from under leaves,
A carrot pipes, and everyone heaves.
"I'm rootin' for you," shouts the bean,
"Let's plant a party, join the scene!"

The peas, they giggle, bursting out,
"Who's ready for a game? Without a doubt!"
With pots for castles and dirt for gold,
They'll grow their stories, young and old.

So let them frolic, let them play,
In pots of mirth, they'll stay all day.
With laughter echoing through the room,
These leafy dreams will never gloom.

Hidden Blooms

Behind the curtain, blooms awake,
A shy little flower giggles in flake.
"Peek-a-boo!" says the tiny sprout,
"We're playing hide-and-seek, no doubt!"

The tulips wear their brightest shoes,
While violets hiss, "We've got the blues!"
Yet sunflowers stand tall with flair,
They twirl and spin, with flower hair.

In the shadows, whispers bloom,
"The petals are out to conquer gloom!"
Cacti chime in—not a soul is lost,
"But watch your pins, it's a prickly cost!"

So let them flourish, rich and grand,
In this indoor world, hand in hand.
With every laugh and every cheer,
They'll grow anew, year after year.

The Quietude of Petals

In silence deep, the petals yawn,
"Rise and shine, it's time for dawn!"
The daisies giggle, twirling about,
While the roses whisper, "Let's break out!"

A donut plant claims it's quite sweet,
"Just don't eat me! I'm not a treat!"
With marigolds cracking jokes on the side,
And geraniums snickering, blooming with pride.

The leaves all rustle; it's quite the tease,
"Who's making noise? With such grace and ease?"
While pots echo with laughter and hues,
In this little world, no room for blues.

So here they sway, each glimmering sprout,
In the quietude, they dance about.
A funny twist in a world of green,
Where every leaf has a joke unseen.

The Secret of Sunlit Corners

In a pot sits a rogue basil,
Chasing light like a toddler's chase.
Mint's getting sassy, what a rascal,
In this funny little plant race.

Spider plants swing with glee,
From shelf to shelf, they leap and dive.
Shhhh! Cacti have secrets, you see,
They whisper at night, oh, how they thrive!

Ferns dance in joy while I pot,
A soil-skirmish, a playful plight.
All my dreams are tangled, a knot,
Yet these green pals make it all right.

Silly succulents, stick out their tongues,
Dare me to water, I'll stall and pout.
A comedy show where laughter's sung,
In the coziest greenhouse, there's no doubt!

Green Dreams in Urban Spaces

Concrete jungles, oh so staid,
Yet my windows brim with cheer.
Fiddle leaf figs throw a parade,
While the neighbors just glare with sheer fear.

Herbs are busy plotting schemes,
In pots that dance upon my sill.
Basil writes novels, dill steals dreams,
And thyme insists he's just too chill.

An avocado perches with flair,
Hoping to sprout an entire tree.
While I sip tea and wildly stare,
At this green sitcom, it's all for me!

From tiny seeds come tales of mirth,
Indoor life's a comic goldmine.
With every sprout, there's boundless worth,
A circus of green, heavenly and divine!

Petals Beneath Glass

A jar holds blooms, my proudest feat,
With petals as vibrant as a prank.
They giggle softly, oh, what a treat,
As I shake the jar, they start to crank!

Ladybugs hold meetings in there,
Debating who gets the best leaf spot.
Their tiny voices fill the air,
Doesn't matter that they're just a lot!

With every shake, they roll and sway,
These posh blooms, throw shade with style.
Their fancy shoes are on display,
Oh dear, they've planned a fashion trial!

Cacti peek in, like wise old sages,
Sipping sunbeams like sweet tea.
They're the guardians of all the pages,
In this vibrant book of glee!

Soft Stems and Silent Spaces

In the quiet, stems do chatter,
Blades of grass whisper in the gloom.
A potted panda cheering, 'What's the matter?'
While I plot more blooms to vacuum!

The snake plant lingers, shunned by critters,
It's the grumpy old man of the bunch.
"Leave my peace!" it quietly mutters,
As I giggle at the indoor brunch!

Every leaf holds tales untold,
Of mischief during the moonlit night.
They play hide-and-seek, brave and bold,
Underneath the glow, quite a sight!

So here in this leafy chamber,
I find joy in their leafy cheer.
With each petal and soft little anchor,
The funniest show happens right here!

www.ingramcontent.com/pod-product-compliance
Lightning Source LLC
Chambersburg PA
CBHW070316120526
44590CB00017B/2701